GALE
CENGAGE Learning

# Novels for Students, Volume 13

**Staff**

**Editor**: Elizabeth Thomason.

**Contributing Editors**: Anne Marie Hacht, Michael L. LaBlanc, Ira Mark Milne, Jennifer Smith, Carol Ullmann.

**Managing Editor, Content**: Dwayne D. Hayes.

**Managing Editor, Product**: David Galens.

**Publisher, Literature Product**: Mark Scott.

**Literature Content Capture**: Joyce Nakamura, *Managing Editor*. Sara Constantakis, *Editor*.

**Research**: Victoria B. Cariappa, *Research Manager*. Sarah Genik, Ron Morelli, Tamara Nott, Tracie A. Richardson, *Research Associates*. Nicodemus Ford, *Research Assistant*.

**Permissions**: Maria Franklin, *Permissions Manager*. Kim Davis, *Permissions Associate*.

**Manufacturing**: Mary Beth Trimper, *Manager, Composition and Electronic Prepress*. Evi Seoud, *Assistant Manager, Composition Purchasing and Electronic Prepress*. Stacy Melson, *Buyer*.

**Imaging and Multimedia Content Team**: Barbara Yarrow, *Manager*. Randy Bassett, *Imaging Supervisor*. Robert Duncan, Dan Newell, Luke Rademacher, *Imaging Specialists*. Pamela A. Reed, *Imaging Coordinator*. Leitha Etheridge-Sims, Mary Grimes, David G. Oblender, *Image Catalogers*. Robyn V. Young, *Project Manager*. Dean Dauphinais, *Senior Image Editor*. Kelly A. Quin, *Image Editor*.

**Product Design Team**: Pamela A. E. Galbreath, *Senior Art Director*. Michael Logusz, *Graphic Artist*.

**Copyright Notice**

of the publisher and verified to the satisfaction of the publisher will be corrected in future editions.

This publication is a creative work fully protected by all applicable copyright laws, as well as by misappropriation, trade secret, unfair competition, and other applicable laws. The authors and editors of this work have added value to the underlying factual material herein through one or more of the following: unique and original selection, coordination, expression, arrangement, and classification of the information. All rights to this publication will be vigorously defended.

Copyright © 2002
Gale Group
27500 Drake Rd.
Farmington Hills, MI 48331-3535

ISBN 0-7876-4896-5
ISSN 1094-3552

Printed in the United States of America.
10 9 8 7 6 5 4 3 2 1

# Nectar in a Sieve

## Kamala Markandaya

## 1954

## Introduction

*Nectar in a Sieve* is Kamala Markandaya's first novel to be published although it is actually the third novel she wrote. It became a best-seller around the world and was translated into seventeen languages. In 1955, it was named a Notable Book by the American Library Association.

The novel was published in 1954, less than a decade after India won its independence from Britain. *Nectar in a Sieve* is clearly influenced by this event, portraying some of the problems encountered by the Indian people as they dealt with the changing times. Markandaya never mentions a specific time or place, however, which gives the story universality. Some of the struggles that the main character, Rukmani, faces are the result of the changing times, but they are the kinds of struggles (poverty, death, loss of tradition) that are experienced by many people for many reasons.

Far beyond its political context, the novel is appealing to modern readers for its sensitive and moving portrayal of the strength of a woman struggling with forces beyond her control. It is a story about the resilience of the human spirit and the importance of values.

# Author Biography

Kamala Purnaiya Taylor, who often writes under the name Kamala Markandaya, was born in Bangalore, India, in 1924. Her family was Brahmin, the highest caste in Hindu society. Markandaya made an effort to know not just the city in which she lived, but also the rural areas. She was educated at the University of Madras in Chennai, India, and worked briefly for a weekly newspaper before emigrating to England in 1948. There she met her husband, with whom she lives today in London. They have one daughter.

Markandaya has made England her home, but she has made many visits to India over the years, returning to stay in touch with her culture and to find inspiration and information for her fiction. As a writer, Markandaya is respected for her accessible writing style and the range of experience expressed in her novels. Critics generally commend her portrayals of personal relationships, social consciousness, and the desire for independence.

While *Nectar in a Sieve* tells the story of a peasant woman facing an array of difficulties, Markandaya's other novels range in subject matter from the middle class to the urban poor to the struggle between Western and Indian ideas and ways of life. Because her own life does not include all of these experiences, Markandaya has been criticized by some Indian reviewers for a lack of true connection to the poor. Other critics accuse Markandaya of losing touch with her identity by living in England. Markandaya's response is that her adult life in England—her choice to be an outsider —gives her an objective perspective on her native culture.

# Plot Summary

## *Part One*

*Nectar in a Sieve* is a first-person narrative told by Rukmani, the widow of a poor tenant farmer in India during the early 1950s. She begins her story with her marriage to Nathan. The marriage is arranged, and because Rukmani is the fourth daughter and there is very little dowry, her best match is to a poor rice farmer. She begins her life with him and finds him to be very kind and loving. He is so understanding that he is not threatened by her ability to read and write.

Soon, she gives birth to their first child, a daughter named Irawaddy ("Ira"). She is worried, however, when many years pass and no more children come. Just prior to her mother's death, Rukmani meets the man caring for her mother, a Western doctor named Kennington ("Kenny"). She talks to him about her inability to conceive, and he helps her. Rukmani never tells Nathan that the reason she gives birth to four sons in four years is because of Kenny's help. The family is very happy, despite having little food or money.

Years later, a tannery is built in the small village where Rukmani and her family live. While many villagers welcome it, Rukmani is resistant because of the changes it brings to the community. When her two oldest sons go to work in the tannery, she is forced to accept it.

Ira is now fourteen and old enough to marry. Rukmani has a matchmaker find a good husband, even though there is a small dowry. A favorable match is made, and Ira moves to the home of her husband.

Five years later, a terrible monsoon destroys Rukmani's home and rice paddy. For a long time, they survive on very little food. Unfortunately, Ira's husband returns her because she has failed to give him any children. Rukmani arranges for Kenny to provide infertility treatment for Ira, but Ira's husband has already taken another wife.

Rukmani gives birth to another child, a boy named Ruki. Ira nurtures him, and when lack of food threatens his life, Ira becomes a prostitute to earn money to feed him. Still, the child dies.

Meanwhile, Rukmani's sons have lost their jobs in the tannery and decide to answer a call for laborers on tea plantations on the island of Ceylon. Another of Rukmani's sons has taken a job far away as a servant.

When a drought hits, the family struggles once again. Rukmani and Nathan are forced to sell everything they have of value just to buy food for the family. When the rain finally comes, it is too late for that year's crop.

One of the neighbors' wives, Kunthi, arrives at Rukmani's house, demanding rice and threatening to tell Nathan about Rukmani's secret visits to Kenny.

Afraid that Nathan will not understand that the visits were for Ira's infertility, Rukmani gives Kunthi some rice, even though it means that her own family will have too little. Rukmani learns that Kunthi also blackmails Nathan for rice, threatening to tell Rukmani that two of Kunthi's sons were fathered by Nathan.

One of Rukmani's sons is killed at the tannery for trying to steal a pelt to sell. Soon after, the paddies are finally harvested, and the family has money again. The youngest of Rukmani's sons, Selvam, breaks the news that he is not interested in a life of farming and has decided to accept a job with Kenny at the new hospital which is being built.

Ira becomes pregnant and gives birth to an albino child. Rukmani knows that, as hard as life would have been for Ira, it will be more difficult with an illegitimate child whose appearance frightens many of the villagers. Selvam loves the child and supports his sister.

The man who owns the land Nathan works informs them that he is selling the land to the tannery owner. Nathan is almost fifty years old and knows no other life but farming. Having few choices, Rukmani and Nathan decide to go find their son Murugan (who is a servant far away) and live with him and his wife.

## *Part Two*

Rukmani and Nathan take the hundred-mile journey to find Murugan. When they arrive, they find that he changed jobs two years previously. When they go to find him, they meet his wife. She tells them that he has abandoned her, and now she must work as a housekeeper to support herself and her children. Rukmani and Nathan have no place to stay, and their possessions and money have been stolen, so they go to the temple where beggars are fed once every day and given a place to sleep. They meet a boy named Puli, who is a streetwise orphan. He shows them where they can break stones for money, and they eventually save enough to return home. Unfortunately, Nathan collapses before they leave and dies.

Rukmani returns to her village, bringing Puli with her, and stays with Selvam and Ira. She is exhausted upon arrival and simply tells them that Nathan died peacefully.

## *Arjun*

Rukmani's first son, Arjun is an energetic boy who grows into an impassioned man. He and his brother Thambi go to work in the tannery, but when they organize the workers in an effort to demand more money, they lose their jobs. Because money beyond what the young men can earn locally is so necessary to a decent standard of living, he and Thambi take jobs on the distant island of Ceylon and are never seen again.

## *Biswas*

Biswas is the moneylender in town and the only character who never seems to suffer from a lack of resources. Rukmani finds him untrustworthy and unpleasant because of his flippant manner of speaking and his suggestions that Rukmani and Kenny have an inappropriate relationship. Because Biswas has money, Rukmani sells him some of her garden produce, and she has no choice but to go to him when she has to sell her fine saris.

## *Ira*

*See* Irawaddy

# Irawaddy

Irawaddy ("Ira") is Rukmani's only daughter. She is beautiful, hard-working, and nurturing. She is married at the age of fourteen but fails to produce children and so is returned home. She cares for her baby brother Kuti in a maternal way, resorting to prostitution to earn money to feed him. Later, she becomes pregnant and gives birth to an albino son Sacrabani, whose abnormalities she seems not to see. She sees him with a mother's eyes and resents the hurtful comments made by some of the villagers.

# Kali

Kali is the wife of a farmer who works a neighboring field. She is very gracious to Rukmani when she has her daughter, helping her through labor and taking care of the house while she recovers. Although she likes to exaggerate stories and is a bit gullible, Kali is likeable and loved by Rukmani. In later years, however, the women drift apart and when Kali arrives to see Ira's baby, she makes rude remarks. The years seem to have stripped her of her sensitivity and kindness.

# Kennington

Kennington ("Kenny") is the white doctor in town who provides modern medical care for the poor people of the village. He is not there year-round, however; he explains that he can only stand to be there for certain spans of time. He becomes frustrated with many of the local customs and seeing so much poverty weakens his spirit. Kenny cares for Rukmani's mother in her last days and then addresses Rukmani's infertility problem. Rukmani is forever grateful, and Kenny becomes a friend of the family. When he visits, he sometimes brings milk or food. He helps one son secure a job as a servant in a distant city, and offers another son a job as an assistant in a new hospital that is being built.

Little is said about Kenny's own family, except that he has a wife and children whom he refuses to allow to restrict his "come and go" lifestyle. At one point in the novel, he tells Ruk that his wife has left him. He seems saddened by this, but his is a solitary way of life, and he accepts loneliness. Kenny's calling is to treat the sick and help the poor as evidenced by the way he raises funds for the hospital while he is gone from the village.

## Kenny

*See* Kennington

## Kunthi

Kunthi is the wife of a neighbor. When Rukmani first arrives in the village, Kunthi is distant and rather unwelcoming. Still, Rukmani stays with her when she is in labor with her first child. When the tannery is built, Kunthi takes advantage of her good looks and attractive figure to make money by entertaining men. She soon gains a reputation and later loses her husband. On the brink of starvation, she resorts to blackmailing Rukmani and Nathan separately to take some of their precious rice. She blackmails Rukmani by threatening to tell Nathan about her secret trips at night to see Kenny. (Rukmani does not want her husband to know that the Western doctor is treating her for infertility.) She also blackmails Nathan by threatening to reveal to Rukmani that two of her sons are his. Her character and bleak circumstances have made her a pitiful and desperate woman.

## *Kuti*

Rukmani's sixth son, Kuti is much younger than his siblings. He is born after his sister Ira returns home, and she cares for him like a mother. He is severely weakened by the lack of food brought on by the drought, and, even though Ira prostitutes herself to earn money to buy him food, he dies.

## *Murugan*

Rukmani's third son, Murugan takes a job a hundred miles away as a servant. He rarely writes to his family, so when his parents try to find him, they discover that he left the job as a servant years previously. When they go to his house, they meet his wife, who tells them he abandoned her for a life of women and gambling and that he never writes.

## Nathan

Nathan is Rukmani's husband. His real name is never given; Rukmani explains that she will simply call him by this name because it is inappropriate for a woman to call her husband anything but "husband."

Nathan is an extremely hard-working man who is dedicated to supporting his family to the best of his ability. Before he brings his new wife home, he builds a new mud hut for her with his own hands. He is poor and merely rents the farmland that he works, never earning enough to be able to buy his own land. His marriage to Rukmani is arranged, but he truly loves her and treats her with affection and respect. He does not discourage her reading and writing, and rarely discourages her from speaking her mind. He is a good companion for Rukmani because when she is stubborn or passionate about something, he advises her in a calm and wise way without discounting her feelings. He is equally loving to his children, and, although he is disappointed that none of his sons chooses to take up farming, he does not impede them in pursuing their goals.

## Old Granny

Old Granny is a kind woman who sells guavas and peanuts on the street in town. She buys some of Rukmani's garden produce but also understands when Rukmani must sell it to those who can pay higher prices. When it is time for Ira to marry,

Rukmani chooses Old Granny as the matchmaker. Despite Ira's small dowry, Old Granny is able to make a good match, and everyone in town is impressed. After Ira and her husband separate, Old Granny feels responsible for what happens to Ira. Although she has almost no money, she gives a rupee to Ira's albino baby. Old Granny is a poor woman who lives on the street. In the end, unable to survive the drought, she dies of starvation.

## Puli

Puli is an orphan boy whose fingers are missing due to a disease. He is cunning, streetwise, and opportunistic. Rukmani and Nathan meet him when they go in search of their son, and Puli helps them find ways to make money to get back home. Puli agrees to go with Rukmani, who provides him with a home and medical care for his skin condition.

## Raja

Rukmani's fourth son, Raja is killed by a watchman at the tannery after he is caught trying to steal a pelt to sell for money. The family is on the brink of starvation, so they assume he only meant to try to feed them.

## Rukmani

The narrator of the story, Rukmani is the widow of a poor tenant farmer. She tells the story of how she came to marry him and of the many struggles they faced over the years. Rukmani is literate, which is unusual for a woman in her position, and she teaches her children to read and write. Sensitive and loving, Rukmani quickly adapts to life as a poor man's wife and helps with the work in the rice paddy. She also grows her own garden to provide additional food for her family or, when necessary, something she can sell in town for money. Rukmani never complains about the poverty in which she lives, but she is vocal when she does not agree with something that happens in her community. When the tannery comes, for example, she makes her disapproval very clear to her friends and family. Still, once she realizes that she cannot change something (like the presence of the tannery), she accepts it.

Rukmani loves her family above all else and worries about her children as they leave home. As much as she despises Ira's prostitution, she never loves her any less for doing it. When her sons announce that they are leaving the village to take jobs in distant places, she is saddened but makes no real effort to stop them.

Rukmani is also a religious woman, participating in the Hindu festivals and praying to the gods. She makes offerings to the gods and goddesses when she prays to them, as is the custom.

What is most striking about Rukmani is her acceptance of extraordinarily bad luck. Whether suffering a drought, a monsoon, or being stranded in an unfamiliar city with no money, she never allows herself to wallow in self-pity. She feels despair and frustration just as anyone would, but her reaction to crisis is to think of a plan to solve it. When necessary, she can be assertive and strong, such as when she fights her way to the front of the line for food at the temple.

## Sacrabani

Sacrabani is Ira's albino son.

## Selvam

Rukmani's fifth son, Selvam reads more than his siblings do. This is partly why Kenny chooses to train him as his assistant in the new hospital. After the hospital opens, Selvam begins seeing patients with minor ailments. He is very protective of his sister Ira and her baby and offers to care for them when Rukmani and Nathan lose their farmland.

## Thambi

Rukmani's second son, Thambi joins his brother Arjun to work in the tannery and later in Ceylon.

## Themes

## *Change*

Rukmani experiences the changes typical of a young woman in her time. She marries a man she does not know, becomes a mother, and, as she has more children, learns to share limited resources with more people.

Other changes, however, prove more difficult to accept. When the tannery comes to her town, she is deeply resistant to its effects on the village and its people. She comments, "Change I had known before, and it had been gradual.... But the change that now came into my life, into all our lives, blasting its way into our village, seemed wrought in the twinkling of an eye." To her, the tannery is destructive to their peaceful way of life, causes prices to increase, and encourages people to choose wayward paths. Although she eventually takes her husband's advice to be flexible, she does so only because she has little choice.

Getting used to change becomes a necessity in Rukmani's life. By the end of the story, her sons have grown and started their own lives, leaving her with an all but empty household. After her married daughter is returned by her husband for not bearing children, Rukmani considers Nathan's advice to get used to it, because it is out of their control. She says:

It is true, one gets used to anything. I had got used to the noise and the smell of the tannery; they no longer affected me. I had seen the slow, calm beauty of our village wilt in the blast from town, and I grieved no more; so now I accepted the future and Ira's lot in it, and thrust it from me; only sometimes when I was weak, or in sleep while my will lay dormant, I found myself rebellious, protesting, rejecting, and no longer calm.

Later, when Nathan loses his land, Rukmani faces the daunting prospect of a completely new lifestyle, begun when she is well into adulthood. Looking for one of their sons, Rukmani and Nathan confront the challenges and hardships of a large, unforgiving city. To make matters worse, their son is gone and they have lost all of their possessions and money, forcing them to devise a new plan to earn money for passage back to their village.

Their lives are in complete upheaval, and Rukmani reacts by adapting and remaining as optimistic as possible, rather than by giving up altogether. When her husband dies, Rukmani must deal with the profound change of going from wife to widow. Markandaya demonstrates through these drastic changes that Rukmani's life is characterized by uncertainty and instability, but because she establishes constancy within herself, she is able to handle the many changes and surprises that come her way.

## *Adversity*

Rukmani faces many difficulties in her adult life. From the time she arrives at her husband's humble mud hut, she knows that life will be more difficult than she imagined. Her new life requires hard work for little money and few comforts. She finds herself the wife of a poor tenant farmer, but takes comfort in the realization that she is happily married to a man who loves her deeply.

When many childless years pass after the birth of their daughter, Rukmani faces the possibility of carrying a social stigma. She solves her problem by visiting Kenny, the foreign doctor in town, whose new methods would not be acceptable to Rukmani's husband. Although she hates keeping secrets from him, she determines never to tell her husband how she came to bear five sons.

Rukmani faces the adversities of natural disaster when a monsoon destroys much of their home and floods the rice paddies on which their livelihood depends. She watches as her children either suffer cruel fates or leave the village to make their own lives. She and Nathan lose their land, and in the end she is a widow.

Markandaya shows, however, that Rukmani is not a woman who allows adversity to destroy her. She has enough in her life that fulfills her (children she loves, friends, and a happy marriage) to find the will to continue seeking improvement. While she is sometimes struck with despair, she never wallows in self-pity. At the end of the story, she is at peace with herself and her life. She is hopeful and cherishes her memories because she clings to the happiness in her past, rather than to the heartache.

## Topics for Further Study

- At the beginning of *Nectar in a Sieve*, Markandaya offers the following quotation from Samuel Taylor Coleridge: "Work without hope draws nectar in a sieve,/And hope without an object cannot live." What is the significance of this quote to the novel as a whole? How does this quote shed light on the author's concerns, as expressed through the novel? What is the significance of this quote to your own life and your own culture?

- Learn more about Hinduism, paying special attention to traditional gender roles, rituals, dress, food, social customs, and core beliefs. What events in the novel are consistent with the beliefs and practices of Hinduism? What events demonstrate the importance of religion to the characters? In what ways is religion important to the story?

- Learn more about British colonization of India and about India's independence in 1947. Draw comparisons and contrasts between America's and India's fight for independence from the British.

- *Nectar in a Sieve* describes some of the effects of the clash between industrialization and agriculture. Do some research to learn about India's economy today. What percentage of India's people live in small villages and do agricultural work, and what percentage live in big cities? Is industry moving into small towns, as occurs in the book? Can you find information about continuing clashes between these two sectors of the economy?

# Figurative Language

Throughout *Nectar in a Sieve* Markandaya uses a variety of literary devices to bring her story to life. Her inclusion of insightful similes (a figure of speech used to compare two unlike things), well-designed allegories, and vibrant imagery enable Western readers to understand and enjoy this novel whose setting, people, and culture are completely unfamiliar. These devices also help the reader to connect with the events of the book through the universality of the experiences and images.

Markandaya frequently uses similes. When Rukmani recalls running through her garden when she was pregnant, she says, "I realized I must have looked like a water buffalo, running in such a frenzy." In an extended simile, Rukmani remarks,

> Nature is like a wild animal that you have trained to work for you. So long as you are vigilant and walk warily with thought and care, so long will it give you its aid; but look away for an instant, be heedless or forgetful, and it has you by the throat.

During the festival of Deepavali, Rukmani watches in wonder at the brilliant fireworks, noting, "Now and then a rocket would tear into the sky, break and pour out its riches like precious jewels into the darkness."

In a moving scene in which Nathan brings her outside to sit, Rukmani sees her own experience paralleled in the landscape. At this point, she is grateful for the blessings in her life, but is saddened because her children are becoming adults and leaving to start new lives. Markandaya creates a brilliant image, both melancholy and enchanting:

> He coaxed me out into the sunlight and we sat down together on the brown earth that was part of us, and we gazed at the paddy fields spreading rich and green before us, and they were indeed beautiful.... At one time there had been kingfishers here, flashing between the young shoots for our fish; and paddy birds; and sometimes, in the shallower reaches of the river, flamingoes, striding with ungainly precision among the water reeds, with plumage of a glory not of this earth. Now birds came no more.

## Flashback

Rukmani tells her story in the past tense. She is a mature woman, remembering back to her childhood and relating the events of her life. From time to time, she interjects thoughtful observations that come from the reflective nature of her recollection. For example, she tells about the birth of her daughter, remembering how kind and helpful her friend Kali was. She observes,

> When I recall all the help Kali gave me with my first child, I am ashamed that I ever had such thoughts [that Kali did not understand what it was like to have only a daughter, because Kali had three sons already]: my only excuse is that thoughts come of their own accord, although afterwards we can chase them away.

Clearly, at the time of telling the story, Rukmani has chased away her resentful thoughts of her friend. Later, she thinks back on her years of motherhood, observing, "How quickly children grow! They are infants—you look away a minute and in that time they have left their babyhood behind."

## *India's Independence from Britain*

The British had controlled India since the early 1800s, but on August 15, 1947, the Indian Independence Act established the self-sovereignty of India and Pakistan. Hindus lived in India, and Muslims lived in Pakistan, although people were free to travel between the two countries.

After British governmental power was dissolved, India's Constituent Assembly chose a republican constitutional form of government (very similar to the American system). A constitution was drafted, its length exceeding that of any existing body of law in the world. Among the provisions of the new constitution was the abolition of the ancient caste system, which had brought great disadvantages to millions of Indians. The first president was Rajendra Prasad, one of Mahatma Gandhi's (an Indian nationalist, moral and spiritual leader in India's struggle for independence from Great Britain) followers and an experienced politician. A cabinet was also formed, with Jawaharlal Nehru as the prime minister.

The first years of India's new government were both trying and dynamic. India chose to remain neutral during the tensions of the Cold War between the Soviet Union and the United States. This unwillingness to get involved made it difficult to acquire famine relief from the United States when a series of natural disasters (drought, earthquakes, and floods) ravaged India in 1950. The American government eventually approved famine relief in 1951, however, with terms that were acceptable to India's political leaders. Soon after, Nehru organized government programs to encourage birth control in an effort to curb overpopulation. He also designed a five-year plan to expand irrigation and hydroelectric programs for farming.

## *Daily Life in an Indian Village*

In Indian villages, now as at the time of the novel, it is common for extended families to live in the same house or nearby. This arrangement requires patience and respect, as struggles over privacy, responsibilities, and resource allocation are a way of life. On the other hand, families are extremely close, which discourages members from going far away. Traditionally, a woman's role has been to maintain the home, rear the children, cook, and oversee religious and cultural observances. Men earn money to support the family and also teach their sons their trades so that one day they can take over the father's work.

Especially in the past, married couples were expected to have children; if they did not, they would lose social standing and respect. Further, without children, the couple would have limited prospects for the future. The arrival of a child was a celebratory event, but the arrival of a son was particularly joyous at the time of the novel. A son would learn his father's trade and assume the business responsibilities for his father while a daughter could not earn money for the family, yet required a dowry for marriage.

## *Hinduism*

Hinduism is the prevalent religion in India, although Islam and Christianity are not uncommon. Hinduism involves many rituals and the recognition of various gods and goddesses. Festivals such as Deepavali are an important part of Hinduism and provide a communal aspect of the religion to complement deeply personal practices, such as meditation and prayer. To Hindus, the cow is a sacred animal, so they do not eat beef or touch any part of a slaughtered cow. This is an important consideration with regard to the tannery in the novel because it explains why so many Muslims initially worked at the tannery and, in part, why Rukmani was disappointed that her sons went to work there.

## Compare & Contrast

- **1950s:** Girls in India are often subject to arranged marriages at a very young age. They are usually at least thirteen years old, and when they are younger, they often do not immediately move in with their husbands.

**Today:** Although Indian women are gaining more freedom to choose their spouses, the practice of arranged marriage is still quite common. Families often adhere to this tradition to ensure that their children are marrying social equals. The tradition is such a central part of Indian culture that, occasionally, Indian families living in the United States arrange the marriages of their children.

- **1950s:** The diet of a farming family in India consists of rice, lentils, vegetables, and some dairy products. Such families eat little meat because of the expense and also because beef consumption is forbidden by the Hindu religion.
  **Today:** The diet of farming families has changed little over the years; most farming families consume part of what they grow. As in the past, most food grown in India is grown on small farms. Meat consumption is still minimal because of religious beliefs.

- **1950s:** In the novel, Rukmani mentions that the men building the tannery are well paid, earning two rupees per day. By modern conversion, this is the equivalent of approximately four cents; yet the standard of living is so low that this is plenty of money.

**Today:** Since 1951, India has instituted a succession of five-year plans intended to breathe life into the economy. With the exception of drought periods (such as in 1979 and 1987), these plans have been successful. Between 1965 and 1980, the economy grew at an annual rate of almost five percent, and from 1982 to 1992, annual growth was over seven percent. This means that despite population concerns, India's economic situation has improved over the last fifty years.

# Critical Overview

Upon its 1954 publication, *Nectar in a Sieve* was embraced by critics and readers alike. The book was praised for its sensitive and artful depiction of life in an Indian village as it changes in the wake of industrialization and modernization. Western readers found the book accessible, despite its unfamiliar physical and cultural setting. A contributor to *Contemporary Novelists* declared Markandaya "one of the best contemporary Indian novelists."

Critics note that although Markandaya wrote the book in English, the language never seems at odds with the themes or the characters' speech. This is an accomplishment because, although English is one of the official languages of India, it is not the language of daily life, especially the daily lives of poor people such as those portrayed in the book. Markandaya manages to write a distinctly Indian story in a Western language. William Dunlea of *Commonwealth* described Markandaya's use of English as "fresh and limpid, only slightly ornate in stylization."

Many critics were especially impressed by Markandaya's accurate portrayal of life in a rural Indian village. In a 1955 review, Donald Barr of the *New York Times Book Review* wrote, "*Nectar in a Sieve* has a wonderful, quiet authority over our sympathies because Kamala Markandaya is manifestly an authority on village life in India." He adds that, after all, "everything that is of final importance in life can happen in a village." Reviewers comment on how Markandaya makes village existence come to life in the minds and hearts of Western readers, allowing them to look inside the minds of people whose experiences are vastly different from their own. J. F. Muehl of *Saturday Review*, for example, noted,

> You read it because it answers so many real questions: What is the day-to-day life of the villager like? How does a village woman really think of herself? What goes through the minds of people who are starving?

Only a few of Markandaya's contemporaries found the book lacking. Dunlea, for example, commented, "*Nectar in a Sieve* is true without being revealing, promising but not remarkable." Most critics and readers, however, are drawn to the rich cultural landscape, the realistic characters, the well-wrought themes, and the lively language.

Since the publication of *Nectar in a Sieve*, Markandaya has written nine other novels, yet this one continues to be the subject of much critical analysis and acclaim. That female Indian writers today are compared and contrasted with Markandaya is further evidence of her staying power.

# What Do I Read Next?

- Pearl Buck's Pulitzer Prize-winning *The Good Earth* (1931) portrays dramatic political and social change in China during the time of the last emperor's reign. Focusing on the farmer Wang Lung, Buck tells a memorable story of terror, destiny, hard work, humility, and ambition.

- Anita Desai is an Indian writer whose work is often discussed in relation to Markandaya's. *Diamond Dust: Stories* (2000) is Desai's collection of short stories in which her typical sense of setting and character is evident as she tells stories that are both riveting and serious.

- Markandaya's *A Silence of Desire*

(1960) is considered by some to be her best novel. It is the story of a woman who discovers that she is ill and visits a faith healer without telling her husband. The novel deals with tensions between tradition and modernity and between logic and belief.

- Alan Paton's novel *Cry, the Beloved Country* (1948) centers on a Zulu pastor and his son. Set in tumultuous South Africa during the 1940s, the novel offers a sympathetic view of people caught in a time and place when racial injustice was common.

- *The God of Small Things* (1998) was Arundhati Roy's first novel. Set in India, it is the story of fraternal twins from a wealthy family. Roy explores themes of ethnic pride and shame, politics, and independence in a story that is mysterious and compelling.

- S. K. Wall's *Kamala Markandaya: "Nectar in a Sieve," a Stylistic Study* (1987) is an in-depth look at Markandaya's debut novel in terms of style. Wall explores how the author's particular telling of the story is important in the reader's reception of its events and characters.

## Sources

Barr, Donald, "To a Modest Triumph," in *New York Times Book Review*, March 15, 1955, p. 4.

Dunlea, William, "Tale of India," in *Commonwealth*, Vol. LXII, No. 20, August 19, 1955, pp. 500-501.

*Glencoe Literature Library, Study Guide for Nectar in a Sieve by Kamala Markandaya*, http://www.glencoe.com/sec/literature/litlibrary/pdf/ (last accessed July, 2001).

"India," in *Microsoft Encarta CD-ROM*, Microsoft, 1997.

"Kamala (Purnaiya) Taylor," in *Contemporary Authors Online*, The Gale Group, 2001.

Muehl, J. F., Review of *Nectar in a Sieve*, in *Saturday Review*, May 14, 1955.

"Overview: *Nectar in a Sieve*, by Kamala Markandaya," *Literature Resource Center*, The Gale Group, 1999.

*South Dakota School of Mines and Technology Study Guide: South Asia Reading Series, Fall 1998*, http://www.sdsmt.edu/online-courses/is/hum375/southasia.html (last accessed July, 2001).

*Teacher's Guide: Nectar in a Sieve by Kamala Markandaya*, http://www.penguinclassics.com/US/resources/teach

(last accessed July, 2001).

Walsh, William, "Markandaya, Kamala," in *Contemporary Novelists*, 6th ed., St. James Press, 1996, pp. 653-54.

## Further Reading

Bhatnagar, Anil K., *Kamala Markandaya: A Thematic Study*, Sarup & Sons, 1995.

> Bhatnagar's analysis of Markandaya's novels reviews the themes presented by Markandaya throughout the range of settings and characters she creates. Bhatnagar suggests how these themes are drawn from the author's experiences in India and Europe.

Lalita, K., and Susie J. Tharu, eds., *Women Writing in India*, Feminist Press at the City University of New York, 1991.

> This two-volume anthology collects writings of Indian women from 600 B.C. to the 1990s. The editors include critical commentary with this wide-ranging collection of letters, poetry, memoirs, and fiction.

Parameswaran, Uma, *Kamala Markandaya*, Rawat, 2000.

> This overview of the life and career of Markandaya, includes a chapter devoted to each of the author's novels.

Rao, A. V. Krishna, *Kamala Markandaya: A Critical Study of Her Novels, 1954–1982*, B. R.

Publishing Corporation, 1997.

Rao offers a critical look at Markandaya's novels, from *Nectar in a Sieve* through *Pleasure City*.

CPSIA information can be obtained
at www.ICGtesting.com
Printed in the USA
BVOW06s1814170917
495116BV00013B/139/P